REALLY LAME CARTOON PUNS FOR TEACHERS

by

Ed U. Kayshun

INTRODUCTION

Hey, teachers … a fair warning … this book turns common teaching terms into some *really lame* puns.

But, if you have a sense of humor like me, then you are likely to enjoy them.

Some of these puns are better than others. Some I am really proud of (like "3-foot ruler" and "pew-pill") whereas others are a bit of a stretch (such as "na-ledge" and "initial evaluation.") Some are a specific shout-out to the hard-working teachers out there who guide our children to become responsible adults. Some are so abstract that I felt obligated to provide a hint. But one thing is for sure … they are all quite punny. (Yep, you read that right … punny … not funny.)

Thank you to my wife of 14 years and two kids for tolerating my sense of humor. They are embarrassed by, and for, me.

Good luck groaning and moaning at these really lame puns. Don't say I didn't warn you!

— Ed U. Kayshun

TABLE OF CONTENTS

CHAPTER 1

Let's start with some obvious ones.

REALLY LAME CARTOON PUNS FOR TEACHERS

REALLY LAME CARTOON PUNS FOR TEACHERS by Ed U. Kayshun

Spelling Bee

"See? I started with an easy one. You're welcome."

— Ed U. Kayshun

Spring Break

"Obvious ... and really lame."
— Ed U. Kayshun

HERE

➔ Undergraduate

Under-graduate

"Did I warn you that these were lame?"
— Ed U. Kayshun

IQ

Eye-Q

"Still rather easy, eh?"

— Ed U. Kayshun

→ Teaching

Tea-ching

"Ah, now they are getting
a little trickier ... but still lame."
— Ed U. Kayshun

➡ Kindergarten

Kinder-garden

"You see, the garden on the left side
is the 'kinder' garden ...
You're welcome."

— Ed U. Kayshun

REALLY LAME CARTOON PUNS FOR TEACHERS by Ed U. Kayshun

CHAPTER 2

Let's switch to the tools of the classroom.

REALLY LAME CARTOON PUNS FOR TEACHERS

REALLY LAME CARTOON PUNS FOR TEACHERS by Ed U. Kayshun

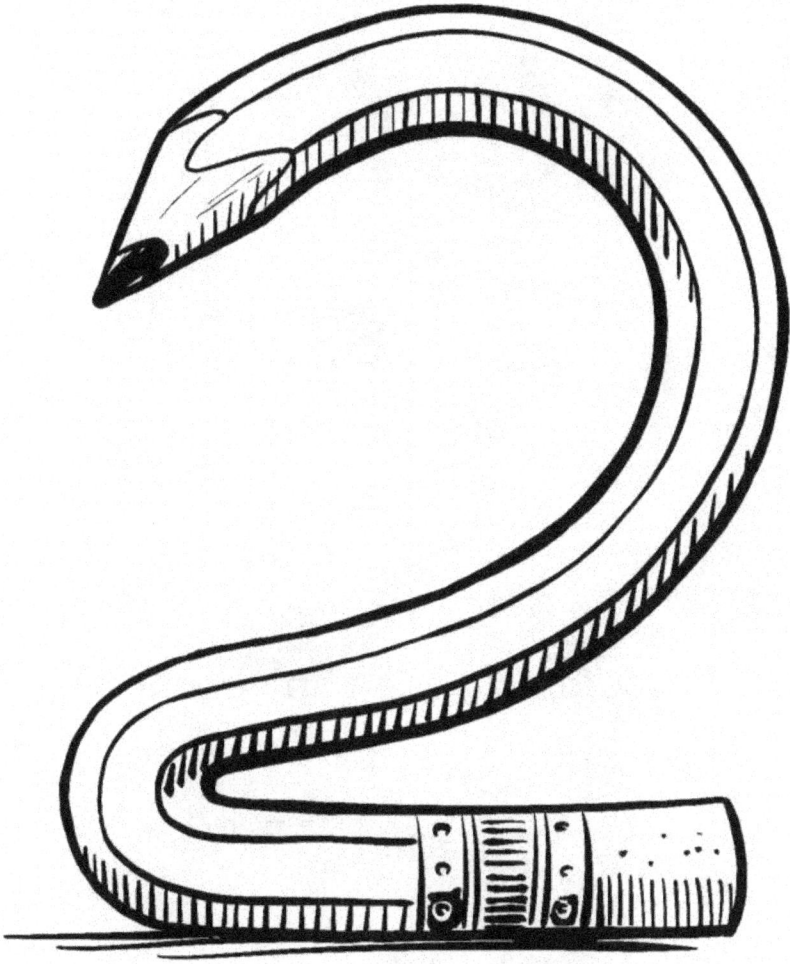

#2 Pencil

"Come on!
If you didn't see that coming,
you should not be teaching."
— Ed U. Kayshun

→ Thesaurus

"Let me explain this one a bit …
They saw Russ …
one of my favorites so far."
— Ed U. Kayshun

→ Notebook

Note-book

"Way too obvious ... and lame."

— Ed U. Kayshun

→ Loose-leaf Paper

REALLY LAME CARTOON PUNS FOR TEACHERS by Ed U. Kayshun

→ Hole Punch

REALLY LAME CARTOON PUNS FOR TEACHERS by Ed U. Kayshun

Highlighter

"You see, that lighter is too high
for him to reach …
making it a high-lighter."
— Ed U. Kayshun

Syllabus

Silly-bus

"Is that a bandage on the tire?
Yep!"

— Ed U. Kayshun

3-foot Ruler

"My all-time favorite lame cartoon pun!"

— Ed U. Kayshun

CHAPTER 3

All about the
trees and the tees

REALLY LAME CARTOON PUNS FOR TEACHERS

REALLY LAME CARTOON PUNS FOR TEACHERS by Ed U. Kayshun

→ University

Universe-tee

"Prepare yourself ...
more lame ones are coming."
— Ed U. Kayshun

ACT

A/C-tee

"You see, that is a
window air conditioner on her shirt.
I know, I know … Lame."

— Ed U. Kayshun

SAT

Essay-tee

REALLY LAME CARTOON PUNS FOR TEACHERS by Ed U. Kayshun

REALLY LAME CARTOON PUNS FOR TEACHERS by Ed U. Kayshun

→ Elementary

Element-tree

"I switched from tees to trees
and didn't warn you. Sorry!"
— Ed U. Kayshun

REALLY LAME CARTOON PUNS FOR TEACHERS by Ed U. Kayshun

REALLY LAME CARTOON PUNS FOR TEACHERS by Ed U. Kayshun

Poetry

Poe-tree

"Um … all of the books
are by Edgar Allan Poe.
Sorry, felt like I had to explain that."
— Ed U. Kayshun

REALLY LAME CARTOON PUNS FOR TEACHERS by Ed U. Kayshun

→ Chemistry Book

K-mystery Book

"Thank goodness
this chapter is over."

— Ed U. Kayshun

CHAPTER 4

Some shout-outs
for EDucation

REALLY LAME CARTOON PUNS FOR TEACHERS

REALLY LAME CARTOON PUNS FOR TEACHERS by Ed U. Kayshun

★ Edward
Edward
Edward

Higher Ed

"You see, that guy on the third floor
is the 'higher' Ed.
I know ... Lame."

— Ed U. Kayshun

Boards of Ed

"One of my personal favorites."

— Ed U. Kayshun

Online Ed

On-lion Ed

REALLY LAME CARTOON PUNS FOR TEACHERS by Ed U. Kayshun

Higher Ed

"Clearly, they should 'hire Ed.'"
— Ed U. Kayshun

CHAPTER 5

Curricula, schools and subjects

REALLY LAME CARTOON PUNS FOR TEACHERS

REALLY LAME CARTOON PUNS FOR TEACHERS by Ed U. Kayshun

Language Arts

REALLY LAME CARTOON PUNS FOR TEACHERS by Ed U. Kayshun

→ Weighted Grades

REALLY LAME CARTOON PUNS FOR TEACHERS by Ed U. Kayshun

Phonics

Phone-icks

"Hmm, that is really lame."

— Ed U. Kayshun

REALLY LAME CARTOON PUNS FOR TEACHERS by Ed U. Kayshun

Magnet
School

REALLY LAME CARTOON PUNS FOR TEACHERS by Ed U. Kayshun

→ Montessori

Monty-sorry

"One of my personal favorites."
— Ed U. Kayshun

STEM
Education

REALLY LAME CARTOON PUNS FOR TEACHERS by Ed U. Kayshun

Parts
of speech

REALLY LAME CARTOON PUNS FOR TEACHERS by Ed U. Kayshun

Baseline
Standards

"Probably the lamest
of them all."

— Ed U. Kayshun

Initial
Evaluation

"You see, those are all
initials on the cards.
I am really sorry about
how bad this one is."

— Ed U. Kayshun

REALLY LAME CARTOON PUNS FOR TEACHERS by Ed U. Kayshun

REALLY LAME CARTOON PUNS FOR TEACHERS by Ed U. Kayshun

Socratic

Sock-rat-ick

CHAPTER 6

All about the people
in the schools

REALLY LAME CARTOON PUNS FOR TEACHERS

REALLY LAME CARTOON PUNS FOR TEACHERS by Ed U. Kayshun

Tutors

Toot-ers

"Yep! That's my favorite!"

— Ed U. Kayshun

➡ Baccalaureate

Becca-Laurie-ate

"Oooh! I like this one."

— Ed U. Kayshun

Principal

Prince-pal

REALLY LAME CARTOON PUNS FOR TEACHERS by Ed U. Kayshun

Principal

Prince-pull

"You should have seen
that one coming."
— Ed U. Kayshun

REALLY LAME CARTOON PUNS FOR TEACHERS by Ed U. Kayshun

→ Pupils

REALLY LAME CARTOON PUNS FOR TEACHERS by Ed U. Kayshun

Pupil

Pew-pill

REALLY LAME CARTOON PUNS FOR TEACHERS by Ed U. Kayshun

REALLY LAME CARTOON PUNS FOR TEACHERS by Ed U. Kayshun

Student

Stew-dent

"You see,
that pot of stew is dented.
I know ... Lame."

— Ed U. Kayshun

REALLY LAME CARTOON PUNS FOR TEACHERS by Ed U. Kayshun

CHAPTER 7

All the ways
we pay for school

REALLY LAME CARTOON PUNS FOR TEACHERS

REALLY LAME CARTOON PUNS FOR TEACHERS by Ed U. Kayshun

→ Scholarship

Scholar-ship

"Too obvious. Too lame."

— Ed U. Kayshun

Welfare

Well-fare

REALLY LAME CARTOON PUNS FOR TEACHERS by Ed U. Kayshun

Tax Levy

Tacks levee

CHAPTER 8

Thank goodness this is almost over.

REALLY LAME CARTOON PUNS FOR TEACHERS by Ed U. Kayshun

Bachelor's Degree

REALLY LAME CARTOON PUNS FOR TEACHERS by Ed U. Kayshun

→ Knowledge

"You see, that is
a ledge on Mount Na.
This one sucks."

— Ed U. Kayshun

REALLY LAME CARTOON PUNS FOR TEACHERS by Ed U. Kayshun

REALLY LAME CARTOON PUNS FOR TEACHERS by Ed U. Kayshun

Reading

Re-ding

REALLY LAME CARTOON PUNS FOR TEACHERS by Ed U. Kayshun

➤ Dismissal

Dis-missile

"And you are now dismissed
from reading my book.
But be sure to check out my
coauthors on the last page."

— Ed U. Kayshun

ACKNOWLEDGEMENTS

I would like to thank all of my wonderful coauthors:

Kerr Rick Ulum
Core S. Werk
C. Lass Ruum
Ped A. Gogy
Stu Dent
Eve Aluation
Becca Laurie Ate
S. Tate Mint
N. Rich Mint
Rhea Meed Eation
Anna Gram
S. Pelling
Chap Terb Ook
Pro Per Nown
Guy Did Reed Ing
Rhea Bus
Sy L. Able
Rhy Ting
Ru Brick
Kon So Nant
Count Ing
Lynn Gwistics
Pho Netik
Dee Code
Stan Za
Sue Doe Nim
Norm Al Ized
Di A. Log
Fic Shin
Graham Er
Prof. Ishency

REALLY LAME CARTOON PUNS FOR TEACHERS by Ed U. Kayshun

REALLY LAME CARTOON PUNS FOR TEACHERS by Ed U. Kayshun

www.ingramcontent.com/pod-product-compliance
Lightning Source LLC
Chambersburg PA
CBHW031536040426
42445CB00010B/558